CAMBRIDGE

Official Cambridge Exam Preparation

CB127929

B1 PRELIMINARY FOR SCHOOLS 2

WITHOUT ANSWERS

AUTHENTIC PRACTICE TESTS

Cambridge University Press & Assessment
www.cambridge.org/elt
www.cambridgeenglish.org

Information on this title: www.cambridge.org/9781108995672

First published 2022

20 19 18 17 16 15 14 13 12 11 10 9 8 7 6 5 4 3 2 1

Printed in Dubai by Oriental Press

A catalogue record for this publication is available from the British Library

ISBN 978-1-108-99964-9 Student's Book with Answers with Audio with Resource Bank
ISBN 978-1-108-99567-2 Student's Book without Answers

Contents

Introduction

This collection of four complete practice tests contains papers from the *Cambridge English Qualifications B1 Preliminary for Schools* examination. Students can practise these tests on their own or with the help of a teacher.

The *B1 Preliminary for Schools* examination is part of a series of Cambridge English Qualifications for general and higher education. This series consists of five qualifications that have similar characteristics but are designed for different levels of English language ability. The *B1 Preliminary for Schools* certificate is recognised around the world as proof of intermediate level English skills for industrial, administrative and service-based employment. It is also accepted by a wide range of educational institutions for study purposes.

Cambridge English Qualifications	CEFR Level	UK National Qualifications Framework Level
C2 Proficiency	C2	3
C1 Advanced	C1	2
B2 First for Schools	B2	1
B1 Preliminary for Schools	B1	Entry 3
A2 Key for Schools	A2	Entry 2

Further information

The information contained in this practice book is designed to be an overview of the exam. For a full description of all of the above exams, including information about task types, testing focus and preparation, please see the relevant handbooks which can be obtained from the Cambridge University Press & Assessment website at: **cambridgeenglish.org**.

The structure of *B1 Preliminary for Schools*: an overview

The *Cambridge English Qualifications B1 Preliminary for Schools* examination consists of four papers:

Reading: 45 minutes
Candidates need to be able to understand the main points from signs, newspapers and magazines and use vocabulary and structures correctly.

Writing: 45 minutes
Candidates need to be able to respond to an email and to write either an article or a story.

Listening: 30 minutes approximately (plus 6 minutes to transfer answers)
Candidates need to show they can follow and understand a range of spoken materials including announcements and discussions about everyday life.

Speaking: 12–17 minutes
Candidates take the Speaking test with another candidate or in a group of three. They are tested on their ability to take part in different types of interaction: with the examiner, with the other candidate(s) and by themselves.

	Overall length	Number of tasks/parts	Number of items
Reading	45 mins	6	32
Writing	45 mins	2	–
Listening	approx. 30 mins	4	25
Speaking	12–17 mins	4	–
Total	approx. 2 hours 12 mins		

Grading

All candidates receive a Statement of Results and candidates whose performance ranges between CEFR Levels A2 and B2 (Cambridge English Scale scores of 120–170) also receive a certificate.

- Candidates who achieve **Grade A** (Cambridge English Scale scores of 160–170) receive the Preliminary English Test certificate stating that they demonstrated ability at Level B2.
- Candidates who achieve **Grade B** or **C** (Cambridge English Scale scores of 140–159) receive the Preliminary English Test certificate at Level B1.
- Candidates whose performance is below B1 level, but falls within **Level A2** (Cambridge English Scale scores of 120–139), receive a Cambridge English certificate stating that they have demonstrated ability at Level A2.

For further information on grading and results, please see the Cambridge University Press & Assessment website at: **cambridgeenglish.org**.

Speaking: an overview for candidates

The Speaking test lasts 12–17 minutes. You will take the test with another candidate, or in a group of three. There are two examiners but only one of them will talk to you. The examiner will ask you questions and ask you to talk to the other candidate(s).

Part 1 (2–3 minutes)
The examiner will ask you and your partner(s) some questions in turn. These questions will be about your personal details, daily routines, likes, dislikes, etc. You will only speak to the examiner in this part.

Part 2 (2–3 minutes)
The examiner will give you a colour photograph to talk about. The photograph will show an everyday situation. You will be given one minute to describe what you can see in the photograph.

Part 3 (3 minutes)
In this part, you and your partner(s) will talk to each other. The examiner will give you a card with some illustrations on it that are connected to an imaginary situation. You will then be given about two minutes to discuss ideas with your partner(s). During the discussion, you should make and respond to suggestions, discuss alternatives, make recommendations and negotiate agreement with your partner(s).

Part 4 (3–4 minutes)
The examiner will ask you and your partner(s) some questions about the topic introduced in Part 3. The questions will focus on your likes, dislikes, habits and opinions. The examiner will either ask you to respond individually to the questions, or to discuss them with your partner(s).

Test 1

READING (45 minutes)

Part 1

Questions 1–5

For each question, choose the correct answer.

1

Mum,
I'm next door at Amelia's. We decided to do some practice for the school concert there – it will be quite noisy, but her parents are out.
I'll be back in time for dinner.
Katy

What does the note say?

A Katy and Amelia have gone to school to practise for the concert.

B There's too much noise at Amelia's house to practise there.

C Amelia and Katy can practise at Amelia's house without disturbing anyone.

2

Sue is texting to

A remind Jenny to find some information for the music project.

B suggest they should meet to talk about the music project.

C recommend a website that will be good for the project.

3

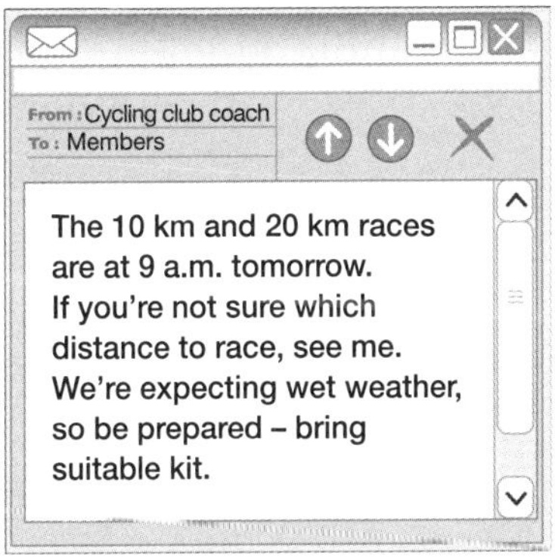

From: Cycling club coach
To: Members

The 10 km and 20 km races are at 9 a.m. tomorrow.
If you're not sure which distance to race, see me.
We're expecting wet weather, so be prepared – bring suitable kit.

What is the coach doing?

A telling members to prepare for the cycling to be cancelled due to bad weather

B warning members that he expects them to be on time for the cycling races

C offering to give members advice on the best cycling race for them to enter

4

Jack,
What time are you getting to Tom's party tonight? Is your mum driving you there? I might be a bit late, so tell him I'll be there as soon as I can.
Melanie

Melanie wants Jack to

A let her know what time something begins.

B pass on a message to someone.

C give her a lift somewhere.

5

From: Mr Thompson
To: Drama club members

I'd like us to have a new logo for our drama club, and I'm offering a T-shirt for the best design! Email me your ideas, and then you can all vote for the best one!

A There's a competition for drama club members to create a new logo.

B The winning drama club logo will be chosen by Mr Thompson.

C The drama club members have decided they need a new logo.

Part 2

Questions 6–10

For each question, choose the correct answer.

The people below all want to visit wildlife parks.
On the opposite page there are eight descriptions of wildlife parks.
Decide which wildlife park would be the most suitable for the people below.

6 

Philippe's family would like to see fish as well as land animals, and listen to talks about the animals. They want to travel there by train.

7 

Asha wants a wildlife park that gives discounts for visiting with lots of friends, and where visitors can have rides on some of the animals. She'd like to feed some animals, too.

8 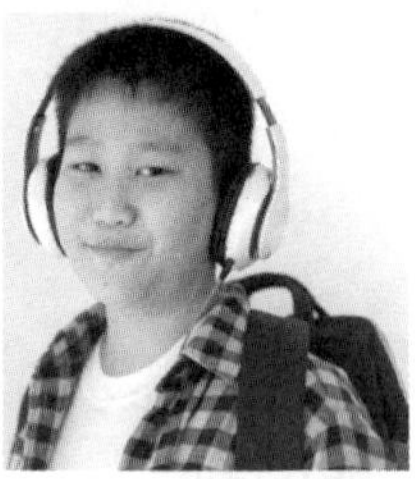

Chanming's family want a wildlife park with activities for Chanming's five-year-old brother. Chanming wants to know what it's like to work at the park, and be able to ask staff questions after his visit, too.

9 

Gabriella and her family want to see animals from all over the world, and be able to touch some of them. They'd like to have a guided tour while they're there.

10 

Kuba and his family want to stay overnight at the wildlife park. They'd like to be able to see some large animals and take home information on all of the animals there.

Eight great wildlife parks to visit

A Hallmouth Wildlife Park

Hallmouth's famous for its large open areas full of monkeys, giraffes and kangaroos! There's also a special play area for younger visitors. Listen to guides and other experts explaining what they do at the park – stay in touch with them by joining their weekly online chat on the park's website!

B Greenway Wildlife Park

At Greenway, you can go around some parts of the park on a horse or a camel! Visitors can also learn what monkeys eat, and even give them their lunch. The animals here are all from Africa and Europe. Cheaper tickets are available for groups of ten or more, and the park is just ten minutes from the train station.

C Rainforest Fun

The main attraction is a huge glass building containing plants from a rainforest, where animals and birds move around freely. Although there isn't really enough to entertain young children or adults for a whole day, it's still an interesting experience. Don't miss the sharks in the building next door, and the larger animals in the rest of the park!

D Jumblehouse Wildlife Park

At Jumblehouse, you'll see many species from around the world, including elephants and giraffes. The shop sells some great books, with details about everything you'll see at the wildlife park. There's so much to do here, you might need two days, so why not book a room at our hotel?

E Naturatastic

Driving up to Naturatastic, you'll see the beautiful 18th-century house and, beside it, the elephants and zebras. There are plenty of staff to show you around and tell you about their work. If you're lucky, you may also see some of the large fish in the lake.

F Kingston Wildlife Park

Just a short walk from the railway station, Kingston's a great place to watch wildlife from around the world, including sharks and many other sea creatures. Every hour, join other visitors in the Kingston Building to hear experts giving information about the amazing wildlife in the park. They can also answer any questions you may have.

G Clifftop Wildlife Park

With creatures from every continent, Clifftop is the biggest wildlife park in the area. It's great for younger visitors – staff will allow them to hold many of the small friendly animals. They take groups around the rest of the park too, and tell them about all the animals. The nearby hotel is great value.

H Bridwell Cross Wildlife Park

The perfect place for learning about animals – there are daily talks about many of the species here. The small farm, where you can feed the sheep and goats, also has rabbits that visitors can pick up. There's a wide range of books about animals available in the shop.

Part 3

Questions 11–15

For each question, choose the correct answer.

I'm Tom, I'm 15 years old, and three years ago my family and I moved into a castle on a small island! It all started when my father was invited to be the castle's manager. He works for an organisation that looks after historical buildings and keeps them open to the public. He was pleased, as he felt he wouldn't be offered such a great chance again, and the rest of us knew this was true, but it was a while before we agreed he should take the job. We were just focused on what life on the island would be like – we knew the castle probably wouldn't be as comfortable as our cosy home just across the water, and there was no school.

Once we'd moved, though, we quickly got used to island life. The castle isn't particularly beautiful, but our apartment in it is comfortable. The island feels very sociable in summer as it attracts lots of visitors, and there are often parties on the beach. During the winter, we only see the other families who live on the island, and there aren't as many teenagers among them as I'd hoped. The adults all support each other, though, and help with repairs on the island, which often involves lots of hard work.

The biggest change for me was travelling by boat every day, back to my old school. I was looking forward to going on stormy days, when there are huge waves – but the ferries don't run then! And I've discovered that if I miss the bus to the harbour after school, I also miss the last ferry home, which is worrying. So when schoolmates come home to stay with me, I'm always telling them to hurry up!

We do get the most fantastic views. Visitors like watching the sun go down over the sea, but I love to see the sun come up. Some days, though, it's so foggy that you can't see a thing, then within minutes it's brilliant sunshine again – it still seems incredible when that happens, even after living here all this time. Of course, we do get awful storms, and I wonder sometimes if the castle's strong enough to avoid getting damaged. But then I remind myself it's been here for centuries – and it's still standing!

11 When Tom's father was offered the job at the castle, his family

A were delighted that he was going to be promoted.

B needed time to decide whether it was a good idea.

C didn't mind leaving their family home.

D didn't realise what an unusual opportunity it was for him.

12 What does Tom say about living on the island in the second paragraph?

A He's disappointed there are so few people his age.

B He's enjoying helping others when they need it.

C He's less keen on the castle now than before they moved.

D He's used to meeting new people all through the year.

13 Tom feels that travelling to and from school by boat

A is the most exciting part of his day.

B means he can't invite friends back after school.

C is still enjoyable even when the weather is bad.

D makes him stressed about getting home.

14 How does Tom feel about the views from the castle?

A He's especially impressed by the evening sunsets.

B He's sad when he sometimes can't see very far.

C He's amazed at how the weather changes so quickly.

D He's worried when he sees storms damaging the castle.

15 What would be a suitable title for this article?

A How we prepared for life in a castle

B Living on an island – the good and the not so good!

C A dream that finally came true

D Do you want an easier life? Then move to an island!

Part 4

Questions 16–20

Five sentences have been removed from the text below.
For each question, choose the correct answer.
There are three extra sentences which you do not need to use.

Jamie Marshall – teenage magician!

Doing magic tricks is not something that only older people enjoy. I've just been in a competition for teenage magicians – and lots of people my age took part. But the best thing was – I won! I did a trick involving taking a ring from someone in the audience. **16** ______ Both the audience and the judges were really impressed by that unusual way of ending the trick.

My interest in magic started with a child's magic set that I got for my birthday a few years ago. I began practising a lot, doing tricks whenever I had a spare moment. **17** ______ But that never happened, and I went on to develop lots of new tricks.

My grandad loves magic, too. He was always doing things like producing coins from behind my ear – his way of giving me pocket money! **18** ______ So he never showed me any of his secrets and I just had to find out for myself!

I also loved performing tricks for friends at school. And as I got better, I started performing at events like family weddings and parties. At first, I thought I'd be really nervous, but in fact, I've always been completely relaxed when I'm performing. **19** ______

What made the biggest difference to my routine, however, was taking up drama classes when I was 15. That really helped a lot. It would be great if I could work in the world of magic when I get older – and even become a famous magician! I'm not really sure what my future will hold, though. I might go into acting instead. **20** ______ That would be cool! But whatever I end up doing, I know I'm going to really enjoy it!

A	And I don't think I'd be so confident now without their help.
B	My parents probably thought I'd get bored with it after a while.
C	Actually, I'd love to be able to do both.
D	I still needed to do some more work on that, though.
E	It's surprising really, as I used to be quite shy!
F	The next time they saw it, it was inside a melon that I'd cut open.
G	It made me start thinking about all sorts of possibilities.
H	But of course, people who do magic tricks never tell you how they're done.

Part 5

Questions 21–26

For each question, choose the correct answer.

Jane Goodall

Jane Goodall is well known for her research into animals called chimpanzees. From early childhood, she **(21)** .... of going to see them in their natural environment in Africa.

In order to **(22)** .... the journey, she did a variety of part-time jobs. When she was 23, she had enough money to visit a friend in Kenya. During her time there, Jane fell in love with the country. She was **(23)** .... a job studying chimpanzees in a national park. At the time, she had no special training for working with animals. She was surprised to find that this **(24)** .... helped her, as she had to **(25)** .... her own way of watching and recording the chimpanzees' actions.

She discovered many new things about the animals, like the fact that they ate meat. Before that, scientists thought they only ate plants, but Jane **(26)** .... that this was not true.

21	**A** imagined	**B** dreamed	**C** hoped	**D** wished
22	**A** afford	**B** pay	**C** spend	**D** earn
23	**A** applied	**B** provided	**C** offered	**D** accepted
24	**A** completely	**B** specially	**C** properly	**D** actually
25	**A** develop	**B** reach	**C** control	**D** gain
26	**A** persuaded	**B** agreed	**C** intended	**D** proved

Part 6

Questions 27–32

For each question, write the correct answer.
Write one word for each gap.

Science-fiction film

Hi Sam,

Have you seen the new science-fiction film, *Rocket*? I was really interested in seeing it because it was based **(27)** .... the book called *Spacemen*, which is **(28)** .... of my favourite novels. To be honest, I always find **(29)** .... difficult when something that I've read and enjoyed is turned into a film, because it's never exactly the same as I imagined! But **(30)** .... time I really wasn't disappointed – the acting was great, and the main characters were very similar to how the author described them in the novel.

(31) .... you haven't seen it yet, why don't you come round to my house and watch it online **(32)** .... me? I know you love science fiction, so it would be great to hear what you think of the film!

Let me know!

Carys

WRITING (45 minutes)

Part 1

You **must** answer this question.
Write your answer in about **100 words** on the answer sheet.

Question 1

Read this email from your English-speaking friend Alex and the notes you have made.

EMAIL

From: Alex

Subject: Running

Hey,

I'm glad you can come to my house to go running with me and my older sister next weekend. — *Me too!*

There's a big park near my house and we usually go there to run for about 5 km. Is 5 km a good distance for you? — *Tell Alex*

My sister and I had planned to pick you up, but her car broke down yesterday. I hope it won't be a problem for you to get to my house. — *Don't worry because …*

We'll probably get hungry. My mum wants to know what food she can make for us to eat. Any ideas? — *Suggest …*

See you soon,

Alex

Write your **email** to Alex using **all the notes**.

Part 2

Choose **one** of these questions.
Write your answer in about **100 words** on the answer sheet.

Question 2

You see this announcement on an English-language website for young people.

Articles wanted!

Learning outside school

What kinds of things can young people learn when they're not at school?
How can these things help young people when they're at school?
The best article answering these questions will win a prize!

Write your **article**.

Question 3

Your English teacher has asked you to write a story.
Your story must begin with this sentence.

I came out of the shop and I saw my friends walking towards me.

Write your **story**.

LISTENING (approximately 30 minutes)

Part 1

Questions 1–7

For each question, choose the correct answer.

---

1 What is the boy's biology project about?

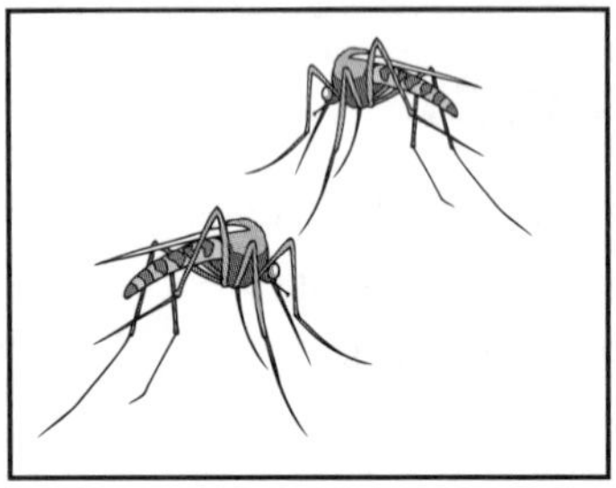

A

B

C

2 Where is the girl's older brother working?

A

B

C

3 Where will the boy and girl meet?

A

B

C

4 What did the girl buy yesterday?

A

B

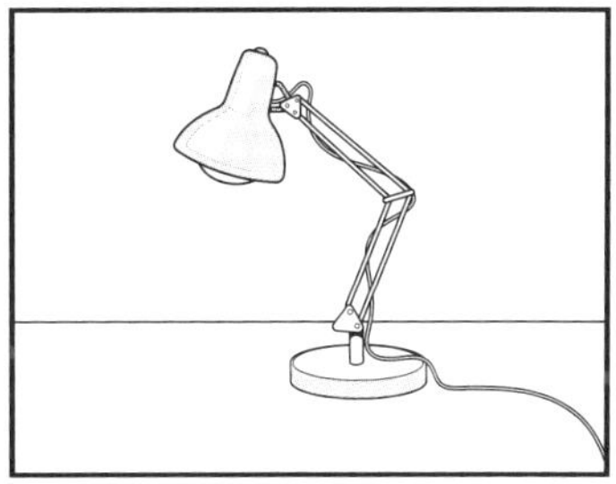

C

5 How will the mother and her son explore the city?

A

B

C

6 What did the boy break?

A

B

C

7 How will the girl's father book tickets for the school show?

A

B

C

Part 2

Questions 8–13

For each question, choose the correct answer.

---

8 You will hear a boy and a girl talking about a film.
They agree that

A the ending was obvious.

B the acting was bad.

C the story wasn't realistic.

9 You will hear a boy talking to a girl about a water sports centre.
What is the boy doing?

A encouraging her to visit it

B warning her about a problem

C complaining about somebody there

10 You will hear two friends talking about playing the piano.
How does the girl feel about it?

A confident about her ability

B relaxed about her progress

C nervous about a future performance

11 You will hear a boy telling his sister about plans for his room.
What does he decide to do to his room?

A have less furniture in it

B replace a damaged piece of furniture

C change the position of some furniture

12 You will hear two students talking about a science lesson.
What are they both doing?

A complaining about what they had to do

B explaining why they enjoyed it

C discussing the purpose of something they did

13 You will hear a boy telling his friend about going sailing.
He is worried about

A how fit he'll need to be.

B what he'll be allowed to do.

C whether he'll forget things.

Part 3

Questions 14–19

For each question, write the correct answer in the gap.
Write **one** or **two words** or a **number** or a **date** or a **time**.

You will hear a talk at a school by a goat farmer called Ben Jones.

Life on a goat farm

A typical goat on Ben's farm produces about **(14)** .... litres of milk a day.

The goats' food contains **(15)** .... grown on Ben's farm.

Ben's son does the **(16)** .... of the farm buildings.

Ben works in his **(17)** .... most of the morning.

Every two weeks, a **(18)** .... visits the farm.

To learn more, see the farm's website: www. **(19)** .... .uk

Part 4

Questions 20–25

For each question, choose the correct answer.

You will hear an interview with a girl called Jenny Baker, who is a young ice skater.

20 What does Jenny say about her morning training?

- **A** She dislikes getting up early.
- **B** She's grateful for her parents' support.
- **C** She doesn't mind missing school lessons.

21 What does Jenny like about her ice skating coach?

- **A** He explains things slowly.
- **B** He makes her work hard.
- **C** He listens to what she says.

22 What does Jenny say about skating in competitions?

- **A** She wants to enter more of them.
- **B** She avoids thinking about prizes.
- **C** She thinks winning proves her ability.

23 When she watches video recordings of her skating, Jenny is

- **A** keen to repeat performances.
- **B** impressed by her progress.
- **C** annoyed by her mistakes.

24 Jenny says that falling over on the ice

- **A** is something she worries about.
- **B** isn't as painful as people think.
- **C** is a necessary part of skating.

25 Jenny says that in the future, she'll

- **A** develop her exercise routine.
- **B** do some training abroad.
- **C** spend more time skating.

Test 2

READING (45 minutes)

Part 1

Questions 1–5

For each question, choose the correct answer.

1

What does the notice say?

A People can only buy drinks at the cinema if they already have a ticket.

B The cinema gives discounts on tickets if customers also buy refreshments.

C There is a special offer available on drinks for cinema customers.

2

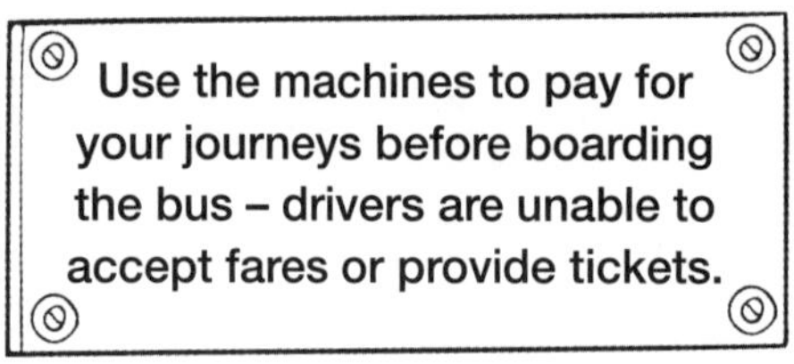

What does the sign say?

A Passengers should buy a ticket then wait for their bus.

B Passengers must get their tickets directly from the driver.

C Passengers have to use the ticket machines on the bus.

3

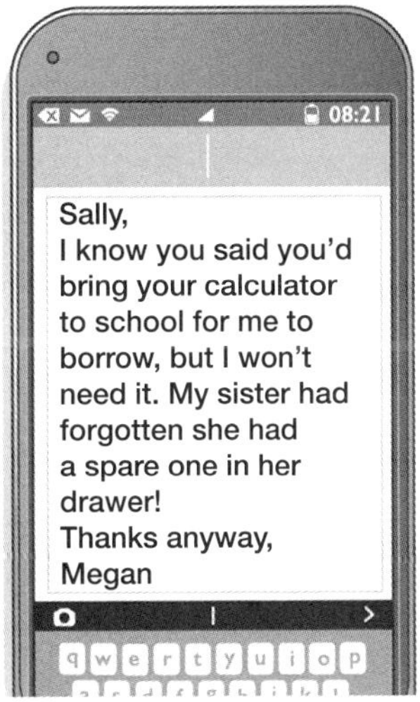

A Megan is thanking Sally for lending her a calculator for school.

B Megan is able to use a calculator that belongs to her sister.

C Megan has remembered where she left her spare calculator.

4

> Don't expect someone else to pick up your rubbish at school! Always use separate bins provided for recycling.

What is the purpose of the notice?

A to remind pupils they are responsible for their own rubbish

B to update pupils regarding the school's recycling rules

C to encourage pupils to collect other people's rubbish

5

> Mum,
> We had a basketball training session today, and I've got a match tomorrow. I know you're doing some washing – would you mind putting my sports kit in? I'll need it for tomorrow.
> Pierre

Why did Pierre write this note to his mother?

A to remind her about an event

B to ask her a favour

C to thank her for something

Part 2

Questions 6–10

For each question, choose the correct answer.

The people below all want to go ice skating.
On the opposite page there are eight descriptions of places to go ice skating.
Decide which place would be the most suitable for the people below.

6  Stephanie and her parents want to listen to music while skating in a city centre. They'd like to buy some skates while they're there.

7  Cameron and his family want to go ice skating somewhere that isn't busy. Although they'd like Cameron's young sister to have a separate place to skate safely, Cameron's a good skater and enjoys skating really fast.

8  Fi and her mum want to skate somewhere where they won't get wet if it rains. Fi wants a lesson with other people, and they'd like to do other activities on the ice, too.

9  Zoe and her family want to go skating in a beautiful location where there's entertainment for Zoe's young brother. They'd also like to see a skating show while they're there.

10  Leo and his family want to find somewhere for Leo to have an individual skating class. Afterwards, they'd like to sit down for something hot to eat while watching other people skating.

Places to go ice skating

A Hamley Hall

Hamley Hall's a 30-minute train ride from the city. With its wonderful gardens by the river and fantastic ice rink, it's a perfect place for a day out. Art and sports classes are also available for kids of all ages. And in the evening, don't miss the *Dance on Ice* performance, with its live orchestra!

B Hill Road

Ice skating at Hill Road, with its spectacular views over the city, is popular with families. Special sessions are available for younger skaters, but everyone must keep to a sensible speed in the general sessions, too. There's a hot drinks machine, and the bus from the city centre stops right outside.

C Langley Skating Centre

Langley Skating Centre is a good place to spend a few hours, with plenty to entertain you. You can pay for a one-to-one session – it's quite expensive, but you'll improve quickly. There's a restaurant right next to the ice rink, so you can get a good view of the action. It's open all day, although it's quieter in the afternoon.

D Ice World

At Ice World, you can do an hour-long skating class – places are limited to ten, so book early. It's worth doing, as it'll give you confidence to join in the games organised there every day – really enjoyable! Best of all, there's a roof covering the whole skating area, so the fun never has to stop!

E City Skate

City Skate is always busy, especially at the weekends, when there's a DJ. If you're not very confident, arrange a lesson for either 30 minutes or an hour. It's fun watching people speed around the ice, and there are good restaurants just ten minutes away. Check the weather forecast, as you'll be skating in the open air.

F Ice Park

Ice Park has a great central location, perfect for families wanting to explore the neighbourhood. Although the large skating area closes at 4 p.m., there's plenty going on in the evenings, too, including the theatre with its great shows, and many fantastic restaurants.

G Chorley Lane

Chorley Lane, located in the centre of the Financial District, is generally quiet, as the area isn't a popular tourist destination. There's something for everyone, though, with a smaller area for kids, and there are fun races for experienced skaters, which is a nice option if you're skating by yourself.

H Devon Park

Devon Park offers great skating, and you can rent everything you need on site. If you're keen, you can get your own equipment here, too. This year, you'll be entertained by bands until late into the evening, when the trees are lit up. It's so magical that you'll forget you're in the heart of the capital!

Part 3

Questions 11–15

For each question, choose the correct answer.

The teenage jewellery maker

Eighteen-year-old Jasmine Holloway writes about how she started her successful jewellery-making business.

When I was 15, I just wanted everything my friends had, and I never planned ahead – for example, I had no idea what I wanted to do when I left school. One day, my best friend got a new phone for her birthday and, of course, I thought I should have one, too. My parents said I could only have it if I paid for it with my own money, so I decided to work part-time and save as much as I could. I owe my parents a lot for making me do that – it taught me a really valuable lesson.

I worked every Saturday in a café, but I didn't really enjoy it, so my parents suggested starting my own little business instead. I'd seen my mum making necklaces for herself, so I asked if I could have a go at that. I'd never imagined I'd find it so easy, as it had seemed so complicated when I'd watched Mum doing it. My friends thought it sounded dull, but I was really into the idea. Mum had shown me it was possible to create something attractive at home using basic tools and materials.

I sold my first items of jewellery to my friends and family as soon as I'd finished making them. They told me they were delighted with them, of course, but I just thought they were saying that to please me. So although I was grateful they'd bought them, I still needed convincing that they looked good enough to be popular with the public.

There was only one way to find out, so I rented a market stall with my mum. There are always lots of tourists where I live, and they bought lots of my things to give to family and friends when they got back home. Soon we were receiving calls from all over the country from people asking to buy more. They thought we were a big business, employing loads of people to produce my designs, when in fact we were just two people on a market stall! That was when I knew it could work, and it was time to take the next step and set up a website.

Since then, I've made thousands of pounds through my business, mostly online, although we still have our stall, too. It's been such a lot of fun so far.

11 Jasmine wanted to save money

A to buy a present for a friend.

B to pay for her future studies.

C to buy something for herself.

D to pay her parents back for something.

12 Before Jasmine started making jewellery herself, she thought she would

A find it difficult to do.

B need special equipment.

C get bored of it quite quickly.

D be unable to produce anything nice.

13 How did Jasmine feel when people bought her first items of jewellery?

A She was disappointed by her family's and friends' comments.

B She wasn't surprised that the buyers were so pleased.

C She was glad that she'd finally managed to sell them.

D She wasn't confident about the quality of her designs.

14 Why did Jasmine decide to set up a website?

A Her jewellery market stall wasn't especially successful.

B People from other areas wanted to buy her jewellery.

C She wanted to work with other jewellery makers.

D Her jewellery company had become so large.

15 What would Jasmine write on the homepage of her website?

A Only available on the internet, my designs are produced by a team of expert jewellery makers, and are of the highest quality.

B My parents taught me all they know about making jewellery and starting a business, but now I run the whole thing myself.

C Having given up my café business to create jewellery, I now have time to make the beautiful products on this site.

D Because of my decision to earn money for myself, I now produce this beautiful jewellery, and I'm very grateful for my family's help.

Part 4

Questions 16–20

Five sentences have been removed from the text below.
For each question, choose the correct answer.
There are three extra sentences which you do not need to use.

The lost camera

Have you ever gone to the coast for a lovely family day out – only to discover when you return home that you've lost something valuable and it's probably still on the beach?

That's exactly what happened to a young British boy called William during a beach trip. He put his camera on top of a rock so that he could make a video of himself and his sister playing. **16** ______ So William and his family went home, with the camera still on the rock. Later, the sea flowed onto the beach and carried it away – about 800 kilometres away, in fact, to an island off the coast of Germany.

The camera was found on the island by the couple who live there. It's a protected area for birds, and no one else is allowed on the island without permission. **17** ______ However, things that the sea has brought in are regularly found there, like fishing equipment and even shoes. But it was still a surprise to find a camera!

Luckily, the camera was waterproof, so the seawater hadn't damaged it. When the couple uploaded its contents onto their computer, they were amazed to see a video of William's beach trip. The last few seconds, however, showed only the water around the camera. **18** ______

The couple put one of the videos onto social media to see if anyone recognised it. **19** ______ Then, amazingly, a special computer programme used for finding boats at sea recognised the exact place in the north of England where William had recorded the video!

A friend of William's read about the video in a newspaper and told the family. **20** ______ William and his father were invited to the island where the camera was discovered to see for themselves where it had finally ended up!

A	But that was exactly what they'd planned.
B	So there's rarely anything left on the beach by visitors.
C	They hoped this would help them to find the person who'd filmed it.
D	But that isn't all he expects to find.
E	It had begun its extraordinary journey across the sea.
F	They were a great success.
G	Unfortunately, he then forgot all about it, and left it there.
H	They immediately contacted the couple.

Part 5

Questions 21–26

For each question, choose the correct answer.

Can dolphins talk?

Scientists know that dolphins are intelligent creatures. But now they are **(21)** .... whether the noises that dolphins make are actually a form of language.

Dolphins make various noises to communicate information to each other, about things like their location in the ocean. But scientists wanted to discover exactly how dolphins communicate when working together. So they recorded the noises that dolphins made while **(22)** .... a difficult exercise. The scientists had designed a box with ropes attached to either side. Inside the box were some fish. The box could be opened more **(23)** .... if two dolphins worked together – using the ropes to pull the box in opposite **(24)** .... to open it.

The dolphins made noises much more **(25)** .... while they were working together to **(26)** .... the problem. But does this mean that they were actually talking to each other? More research is needed before scientists can be sure.

21	**A**	guessing	**B**	wondering	**C**	thinking	**D**	believing
22	**A**	completing	**B**	reaching	**C**	ending	**D**	producing
23	**A**	accurately	**B**	properly	**C**	easily	**D**	correctly
24	**A**	routes	**B**	directions	**C**	paths	**D**	positions
25	**A**	generally	**B**	immediately	**C**	usually	**D**	frequently
26	**A**	answer	**B**	explain	**C**	solve	**D**	deal

Part 6

Questions 27–32

For each question, write the correct answer.
Write **one** word for each gap.

Book review

I've just finished reading Sara Tyler's latest book, *Gold River*. I think that it's even better than her last book. If you're looking **(27)** .... an interesting book to read, then this **(28)** .... the perfect choice.

The main characters are described in a lot of detail, and I really cared about **(29)** .... happened to them. If you're one of the thousands of people who have enjoyed other books **(30)** .... Sara Tyler, you'll already know that some of her novels were made into films **(31)** .... few years ago. I wouldn't be surprised if this happens to *Gold River*, too. Although this book has new characters, **(32)** .... is set in the same place as her other stories, so you might recognise some of the locations. Go and read it – I promise you won't regret it!

WRITING (45 minutes)

Part 1

You **must** answer this question.
Write your answer in about **100 words** on the answer sheet.

Question 1

Read this email from your English-speaking friend Pat and the notes you have made.

EMAIL

From: Pat

Subject: School music project

Hi,

I've been to the library and got a couple of books we can use to help us with the school music project we're doing together. — *Thanks!*

I think we should write about classical music – what do you think? — *Tell Pat*

Shall we use your laptop to work on the project? — *Sorry, but …*

It's probably a good idea to get someone to check our work before we give it to the teacher. Who's the best person to ask? — *Suggest someone*

See you soon,

Pat

Write your **email** to Pat using **all the notes**.

Part 2

Choose **one** of these questions.
Write your answer in about **100 words** on the answer sheet.

Question 2

You see this announcement in an English-language magazine for young people.

Articles wanted!

Free time

When you and your friends are not at school, do you prefer just relaxing at home, or doing organised activities such as going to a club or having sports lessons? Why?

We'll publish the ten best articles answering these questions next month!

Write your **article**.

Question 3

Your English teacher has asked you to write a story.
Your story must begin with this sentence.

Mallory opened the door and ran down the street.

Write your **story**.

LISTENING (approximately 30 minutes)

Part 1

Questions 1–7

For each question, choose the correct answer.

---

1 Which sport will the girl do next term?

A

B

C

2 Which object in the museum did the boy like?

A

B

C

3 What does the boy decide to leave behind?

A

B

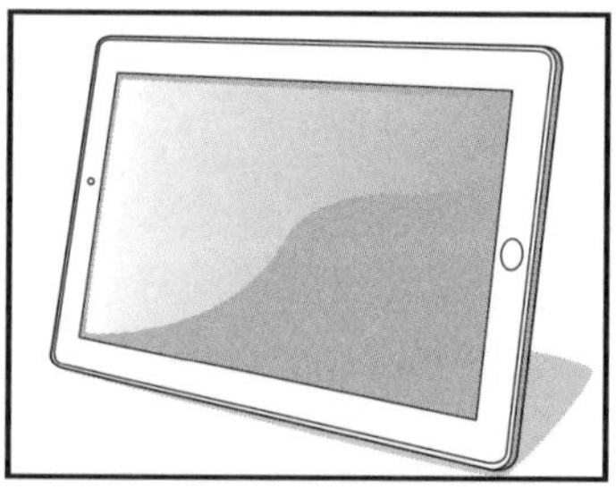
C

4 What is the baby giraffe doing?

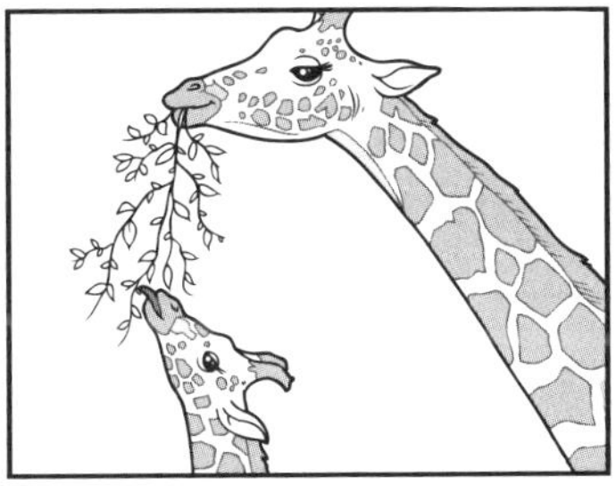

A

B

C

5 What does the boy decide to make in the cookery lesson?

A

B

C

6 Where did the girl go on holiday?

A

B

C

7 How did the boy travel to his aunt's house?

A

B

C

Part 2

Questions 8–13

For each question, choose the correct answer.

---

8 You will hear a boy telling his friend about a school show.
The show is cancelled because of a problem with

A the stage lighting.

B the musicians.

C the main performer.

9 You will hear two friends talking about homework.
What does the girl say about homework?

A Younger students shouldn't have to do it.

B Students should only get it in certain subjects.

C There should be less homework for maths.

10 You will hear two friends talking about a computer game.
What does the boy think about it?

A It has very clear instructions.

B It's challenging to play.

C It's not too expensive to buy.

11 You will hear a girl and a boy talking about a sports centre.
What is the girl doing?

A suggesting an activity

B apologising for a mistake

C reminding him about an arrangement

12 You will hear two friends talking about a party.
What do they agree that they need advice about?

A decorating the room

B choosing the music

C preparing the food

13 You will hear two friends talking about a football match.
How does the girl feel after her conversation with the coach?

A confident that she'll play in another match soon

B curious about why she can't play in the match

C jealous of the girls who'll play in the match

Part 3

Questions 14–19

For each question, write the correct answer in the gap.
Write **one** or **two words** or a **number** or a **date** or a **time**.

You will hear a woman called Mona Dawson talking to a group of students about her work as a news reporter.

News reporter

Mona studied **(14)** .... before she became a news reporter.

Mona's first news article was about a **(15)** ....

Mona never goes anywhere without a **(16)** ....

Mona's next TV interview will be with a **(17)** .... from a large transport company.

Mona thinks it's important for a TV news reporter to have a good **(18)** ....

Mona is going to write a book about using energy from **(19)** ....

Part 4

Questions 20–25

For each question, choose the correct answer.

You will hear an interview with a young man called Matt Luxton, who worked as a volunteer at a rescue centre for sick elephants.

20 Matt heard about the elephant rescue centre from his

A friend.

B mother.

C teacher.

21 How did Matt get enough money for his trip?

A He borrowed money from a relative.

B He worked for a local company.

C He sold some things he owned.

22 What did Matt notice when he arrived at the rescue centre?

A how beautiful all the plants were

B how friendly the people were

C how many elephants there were

23 What was Matt's first job at the rescue centre?

A He prepared the elephants' food.

B He helped the medical staff.

C He washed the elephants.

24 What did Matt find difficult about working at the rescue centre?

A getting up early

B dealing with the temperature

C communicating with people

25 The most surprising thing Matt learnt about elephants was how

A kind they are to each other.

B different their characters are.

C well they remember things.

Test 3

READING (45 minutes)

Part 1

Questions 1–5

For each question, choose the correct answer.

1

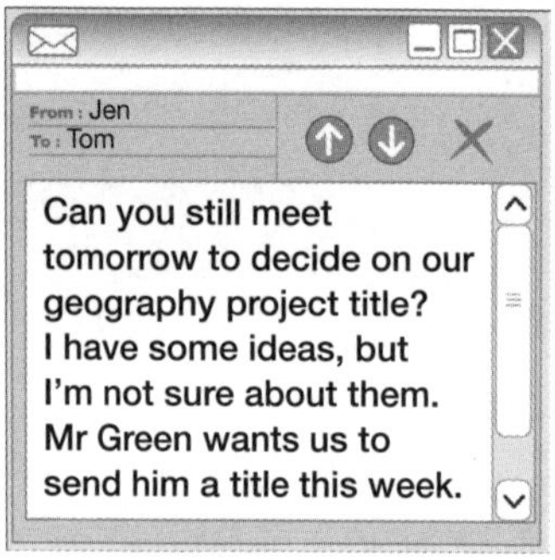

Jen is asking Tom to

A choose one of her ideas for their project title.

B tell Mr Green which project title they have chosen.

C confirm that he can see her to discuss their project title.

2

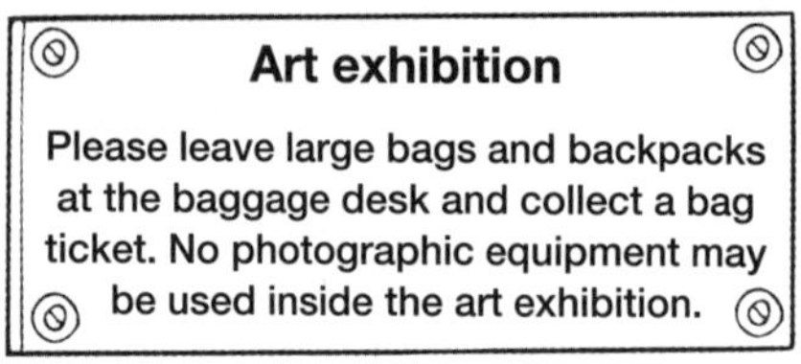

What does the sign say?

A A ticket is needed to see the art exhibition.

B Cameras must be left at the baggage desk.

C Only small bags can be taken into the exhibition.

3

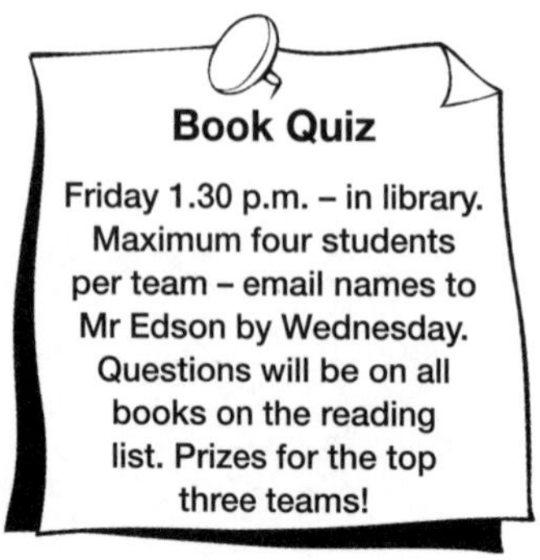

A Students must be in teams of four to enter the competition.

B Students have to enter this school competition in advance.

C Students get a prize if they read all the books on the reading list.

4

Having problems with your schoolwork?
Free homework sessions in the library after school.
Teachers available to help with any subject.

The notice is for pupils who want

A to help their classmates after school.

B some support with their homework.

C more independent study time at school.

5

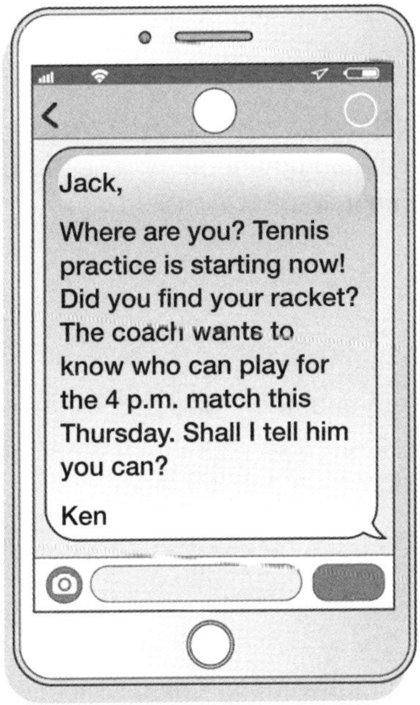

Ken is offering to

A help Jack find his tennis racket for Thursday's match.

B inform the coach whether Jack is available on Thursday.

C explain to the tennis coach why Jack is late.

Part 2

Questions 6–10

For each question, choose the correct answer.

The people below are all doing school projects about the weather, and want to find a website to help them.
On the opposite page there are eight descriptions of websites about the weather.
Decide which website would be the most suitable for the people below.

6 

Sami is interested in how technology is used to predict the weather. He'd also like expert online help on how to start collecting weather information to look for patterns in local weather.

7 

Marcia wants to read about areas of the world that frequently have bad weather, such as very strong winds, and learn about the reasons for it. She'd also like to see photos of these events.

8 

Tom wants to learn how to predict weather changes by looking at the sky. He'd also like to upload his photos of the sky and get advice on improving them.

9 

Lily would like to know how the sea affects the weather across the planet. She wants to see diagrams showing how this happens, and also to contact other weather watchers in different countries.

10 

Joseph would like to meet other teenagers who record the weather. He wants information about changes in weather, such as when it becomes unusually hot, and to learn about ways people can prepare for these events.

Weather websites

A MetBureau

Get clear, helpful tips on how to record daily information about the weather, such as wind direction, amounts of rain and sea temperature. And on this website, you'll also find the work of some professional photographers who have taken beautiful photos of the sky, such as at sunrise and sunset.

B Tempus

This website has clear maps and detailed drawings explaining how the oceans move warm and cold water around, and influence temperature and weather patterns around the world. You can also exchange experiences with other site users all over the world who study the weather!

C Weather Watch

Interested in huge storms and other extreme weather conditions? There's information here about why these take place, and which countries are most likely to experience them. There are also spectacular pictures, like of storms and clouds, taken by people who follow these weather conditions using complex technology.

D Elemental

This website follows changes in local weather – click on the map to see your area! Clear diagrams also show how winds and oceans influence your weather, and explain the weather conditions that produce different clouds. Find details of clubs in your area to meet young people who share your interest, too.

E Weather Eye

This website tells you the ways computers and space satellites watch weather conditions around the world and produce forecasts. Professionals give advice about setting up your own weather station and keeping daily records of wind speed, clouds, high and low temperatures and rainfall in your area, to see if trends are changing.

F Sundial

Weather conditions like storms, and also heatwaves, which bring very high summer temperatures, are happening more frequently. This website explains the reasons and gives tips on how to be ready for them. Find out, too, about clubs where you live, where young people set up weather stations, and look at all the information they've collected.

G MetMonitor

Look inside a modern weather centre, and discover how both computers and studying the sky help with weather forecasts. You'll also find videos of extreme weather like high temperatures, and see how forecasts warn us about these events. Upload weather information you've recorded to share with our scientists!

H Meteo

This website explains how the three main types of cloud form, and what they tell us about the kind of weather that's approaching. Impress your friends when you're out with them and can tell them if it's going to rain! Experts will give you tips to help you make your own cloud pictures better if you share them on the website.

Part 3

Questions 11–15

For each question, choose the correct answer.

Football and me!

Sixteen-year-old Alicia Hughes looks back at how she started out in football.

I started playing football when I was seven. I'd rush home from school to play with other boys and girls. I loved it, and after a while, I wasn't a bad player. However, my family knew I often became keen on new hobbies and then dropped them, so I'm sure they thought the same thing would happen with football. But it never did.

In fact, I was already dreaming of playing football professionally when I was older. And the opportunity came sooner than I'd hoped. I often played in local tournaments, and one of the referees noticed that I was a promising player, so he asked the manager of a professional women's club to watch me play. After that, she asked me to join her club. I didn't believe it at first – I thought they'd got my age wrong, and I had no idea that young girls could join women's clubs. But the manager was impressed, and I started regular training with a big club as a young 13-year-old.

After that, I improved enormously. Despite this, people still weren't sure I'd ever be a star player, which made me feel a bit upset. But the coach encouraged me to just be myself, and believe in myself – he even let me play in one of the club's championship matches, much earlier than I'd expected! I've never run so hard in my life – I didn't want the other players to blame me for losing. Then by pure luck, I got the winning goal. As usual, in spite of the large crowd, I could clearly hear my coach's voice cheering me on, and after the match, the team carried me round the pitch. I felt fantastic!

Since then, I've scored lots more winning goals! And next month, my coach and I are running a football tournament for teenagers in my area. The aim is to give them a chance to chat to the professional players in my club. It'll let them see the professional environment, and encourage them to feel they could play for a top team, if they're prepared to put in the work. But my advice to them will be the same as my coach gave me – you'll have good times, but be prepared for bad times, too. I've had very few of those, though – so I've been lucky!

11 Alicia says that when she first started playing football, she

A immediately discovered she had a talent for the game.

B was too busy with other activities to play very often.

C tried to find more girls to play football with her.

D felt no one believed she'd be interested in it for long.

12 When Alicia was asked to join a women's football club, she was

A convinced that she wouldn't enjoy it.

B worried that the invitation might be a mistake.

C sure that her skills wouldn't be good enough.

D surprised that women's clubs even existed.

13 When Alicia played in her first big club match, she

A was keen not to disappoint the rest of the team.

B felt she was ready to play in such an important event.

C promised herself she would manage to score a goal.

D was embarrassed at the attention she got after the match.

14 Alicia says she hopes that the football tournament for teenagers will

A result in more of them playing for their local teams.

B help her coach select the ones who could become professional.

C show them what they need to do to reach a high level.

D introduce them to teenagers in their area who also want to start playing.

15 What would Alicia's coach write about her?

A

Alicia wanted to prove to other people who said she wasn't good enough that they were wrong – it's great that she didn't take any notice of them.

B

Alicia's produced some amazing performances so far, and helped to win many matches. And I still shout more loudly than anyone else!

C

I'm impressed that Alicia has never given up, even during the many times when things weren't going well.

D

I'm glad Alicia took my advice about needing to change clubs regularly to succeed in professional football. Her attitude's completely changed now.

Part 4

Questions 16–20

Five sentences have been removed from the text below.
For each question, choose the correct answer.
There are three extra sentences which you do not need to use.

Julie Danes, teenage comedy performer

Julie Danes is in many ways like any other 14-year-old. She enjoys having a laugh, and making other people laugh. The only difference is that when Julie tells a joke, she's often in front of an audience of hundreds of people. She's a successful comedian in Boston, in the USA.

Since Julie started as a comedian, her performance schedule has become busier and busier. **16** ______ She thinks that she's probably performed in public about 60 times at theatres all around the city.

Even though she's much younger than most of the other comedians in Boston, she's not in fact the only young person doing comedy on stage there. **17** ______ However, it's really only age that they have in common – Julie says their styles are very different. When she goes on stage, people in the audience are curious about the fact that she's quite young for a comedian. **18** ______ But Julie's act also covers lots of other topics, just like those of older comedians.

When she first became interested in performing comedy, she felt slightly anxious about telling her parents of her plans. **19** ______ Despite this, they still haven't been to one of her shows. They don't want her to feel under extra pressure – she might feel more nervous than usual if they were there.

20 ______ And when that day comes, Julie's mum and dad will make sure they are in the audience. And they'll certainly be very proud parents!

A	And so of course, they all enjoy her jokes about that.
B	Many of these theatres are great places to perform.
C	But when she did, they were pleased, and encouraged her to try it.
D	They've travelled all over the USA to watch her perform.
E	In fact, she now appears on stage about once a week.
F	Another 14-year-old, Brandon Phillips, frequently performs at the same shows.
G	Julie's promised to let them know as soon as she feels ready for them to see her.
H	That's why she likes appearing in front of so many people.

Part 5

Questions 21–26

For each question, choose the correct answer.

What will cars be like in the future?

Cars today are nothing like the ones that were driven a century ago. So it's difficult to **(21)** .... what cars might be like 100 years from now. Because vehicles nowadays create a number of serious problems on our roads, it's likely that future cars will actually be very different.

It's certain that technology will strongly **(22)** .... the design of future cars, with computers becoming even more important. Some scientists and engineers are even **(23)** .... that in the future, there could be some kind of flying car, which will travel several metres above the ground!

Most people, however, agree that cars should **(24)** .... environmentally cleaner, so car companies are likely to **(25)** .... the engines we have now with ones that can use clean fuels and other **(26)** .... of green energy.

21	**A** suppose	**B** realise	**C** imagine	**D** recognise
22	**A** allow	**B** involve	**C** persuade	**D** influence
23	**A** predicting	**B** telling	**C** deciding	**D** describing
24	**A** succeed	**B** become	**C** produce	**D** achieve
25	**A** remove	**B** change	**C** replace	**D** improve
26	**A** types	**B** ways	**C** methods	**D** styles

Part 6

Questions 27–32

For each question, write the correct answer.
Write **one** word for each gap.

Review of Amazing

by Gina Thomann

A new play called *Amazing* is now on at the Town Theatre, and it's really worth seeing. The action takes place in a school, and the play starts by showing a group of students inventing an extraordinary machine. They then use this machine in order **(27)** .... learn about history and other school subjects by travelling backwards through time. **(28)** .... example, they see exactly what happened when important medicines **(29)** .... discovered.

(30) .... the story is extremely interesting, some of the acting is not so good. None **(31)** .... the actors are very well known, and I think the play would be a bit better if it had more experienced people in the main roles.

Despite **(32)** .... , I would definitely recommend you to go and see it because of the fantastic story, and the rather surprising ending.

WRITING (45 minutes)

Part 1

You **must** answer this question.
Write your answer in about **100 words** on the answer sheet.

Question 1

Read this email from your English teacher Mr Lyons and the notes you have made.

EMAIL

From: Mr Lyons

To: All students

Subject: School play

Some students have written a play in English. I'd like some of you to perform it in the school theatre next month.

Great idea!

We need people to act in the play, or help with things like painting the scenery for the stage and making costumes. Can you do anything to help?

Offer …

We want lots of students and parents to come and watch the play. How can we let them know about the play?

Tell Mr Lyons

I'd like to have a meeting to discuss plans for the play. Could you come next Tuesday after school?

Sorry, but …

John Lyons

Write your **email** to Mr Lyons using **all the notes**.

Part 2

Choose **one** of these questions.
Write your answer in about **100 words** on the answer sheet.

Question 2

You see this announcement on an international English-language website for young people.

Articles wanted!

Teenage pop stars

Do you think that being a famous teenage pop star is easy? Why?

What influence can teenage pop stars have on their fans?

We'll publish the most interesting articles answering these questions on our website.

Write your **article**.

Question 3

Your English teacher has asked you to write a story.
Your story must begin with this sentence.

Toby was getting ready to go on a fantastic day out.

Write your **story**.

LISTENING (approximately 30 minutes)

Part 1

Questions 1–7

For each question, choose the correct answer.

---

1 What is the girl going to do this summer?

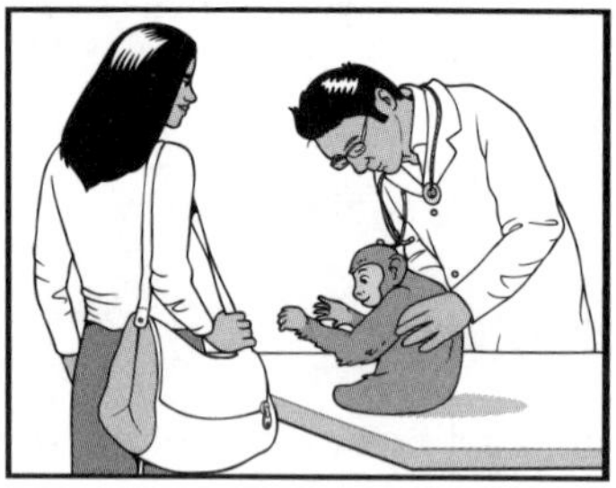

A

B

C

2 Which book did the boy buy?

A

B

C

3 How will the girl get home from school today?

A

B

C

4 What will the boy eat for breakfast?

A

B

C

5 Which lesson has the girl got next?

A

B

C

6 How much were the girl's new sunglasses?

A

B

C

7 Where are the friends going to meet?

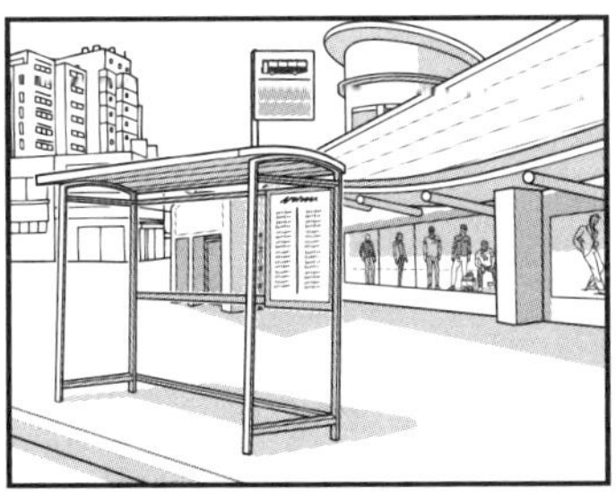

A

B

C

Part 2

Questions 8–13

For each question, choose the correct answer.

---

8 You will hear a brother and sister talking about a train journey.
What do they both complain about?

A the lack of seats

B the behaviour of passengers

C the temperature on the train

9 You will hear two friends talking about going to the cinema.
How does the boy feel?

A unsure which film he'll enjoy

B worried that some films might be boring

C disappointed by the choice of films

10 You will hear two friends talking about a new swimming pool.
What does the girl say about it?

A The opening times are convenient.

B The changing rooms look modern.

C The drinks in the café are expensive.

11 You will hear two friends talking about an after-school science club.
What does the boy say about the club?

A The girl would enjoy attending it.

B There were some challenging activities to do.

C He thinks the teacher is good.

12 You will hear a boy telling a friend about a family camping holiday he went on.
What did the boy find disappointing?

A the location of the campsite

B the evening entertainment

C the outdoor activities available

13 You will hear two friends talking about an accident the boy had.
The boy felt better after

A going to the doctor.

B taking some medicine.

C putting on a bandage.

Part 3

Questions 14–19

For each question, write the correct answer in the gap.
Write **one** or **two words** or a **number** or a **date** or a **time**.

You will hear a boy called Victor giving a class presentation about a boat trip he went on.

Boat trip

The name of the boat Victor went on was **(14)** ....

Victor's boat trip lasted **(15)** .... hours.

Victor saw some **(16)** .... swimming near the boat.

Victor especially enjoyed visiting some **(17)** .... on an island.

Boat trips are available all year except in **(18)** ....

For more information, go to www. **(19)** ....islandboattrips.com

Part 4

Questions 20–25

For each question, choose the correct answer.

You will hear an interview with a young woman called Amy Wu, who makes video blogs and uploads them to the internet.

20 Amy got the idea of making video blogs

- **A** after meeting other bloggers.
- **B** during a lesson at school.
- **C** while she was unwell.

21 What was Amy's last video blog about?

- **A** an exercise routine
- **B** a kind of health food
- **C** a brand of sports shoe

22 Before recording a video blog, Amy says it's important to

- **A** choose the right clothes.
- **B** spend some time relaxing.
- **C** practise what she will say.

23 Every day Amy makes sure that she

- **A** replies to messages from her fans.
- **B** looks at social networking sites.
- **C** writes a personal diary.

24 Who does Amy enjoy interviewing most?

- **A** people who want to change the world
- **B** people who have won sports competitions
- **C** people who most teenagers admire

25 Why did Amy make a video blog called 'My Mistakes'?

- **A** to attract new audiences
- **B** to show she's an ordinary person
- **C** to make her fans laugh

Test 4

READING (45 minutes)

Part 1

Questions 1–5

For each question, choose the correct answer.

1

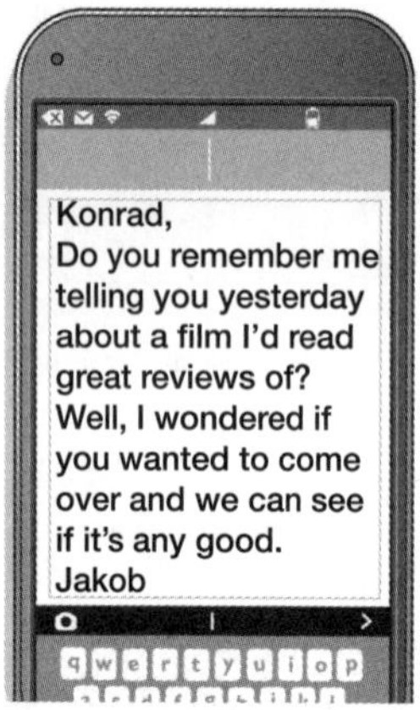

What is Jakob doing?

A telling Konrad about a film he saw recently

B inviting Konrad to watch a film with him

C reminding Konrad that they arranged to see a film

2

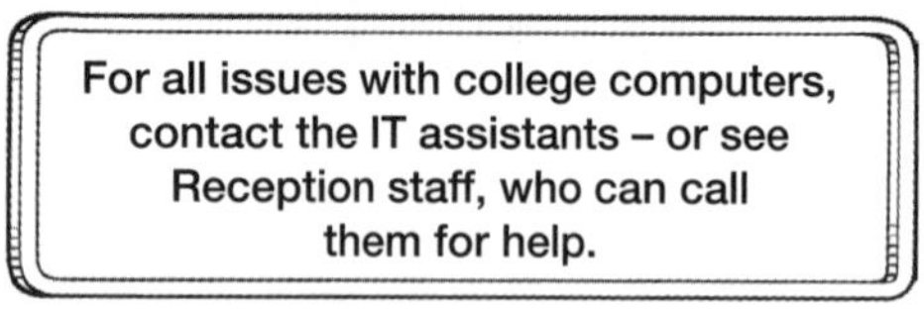

What does the sign say?

A Phone a member of staff for instructions on how to use the college computers.

B IT assistants at Reception can fix the college computers.

C Support is provided for any college computer problem.

3

What can students do at this event?

A improve their story writing skills

B listen to a story read by a famous writer

C advise each other on story writing

4

Park Sports Competition, Saturday
Sign up at café. Free sunhat and water for everyone.
Further details: parksports.com

What does the notice say?

A People taking part must register online.

B Everyone will have the chance to win a prize.

C Competitors will not be charged for water on the day.

5

Why has Jess sent the message?

A to explain to Fiona the reason for a delay

B to check whether Fiona is still coming

C to suggest a different time to meet Fiona

Part 2

Questions 6–10

For each question, choose the correct answer.

The people below all want to find a café they can go to.
On the opposite page there are eight descriptions of cafés.
Decide which café would be the most suitable for the people below.

6 

Kate and Natalie want a small place that isn't usually crowded, where they can sit and chat and have a vegetarian lunch. They'd like a café decorated in a bright, cheerful way.

7 

Tom and his mum want to go to a quiet café for lunch. Tom's mum would like a nice view to enjoy while they're eating, and Tom wants to go somewhere that's famous for its desserts.

8 

Jack and his dad both love sport. They'd like a café that's popular with sports fans, and where they can get great cooked food at a reasonable price.

9 

Sophie and Janine are doing art projects, and want a café where they can see some art and also find something to read while they're having a snack. They'd like somewhere in a historic building.

10 

Maria and Ben often meet all their friends after school. They want a lively café with space for them to all sit outside together, and where the menu changes regularly.

Cafés

A **Tempo** is in an old library building, and serves different dishes every week! The café isn't big, but its plain white walls and windows looking onto the narrow street make it light inside. It's on a popular route for runners, so watch them going past while you enjoy your meal.

B **Marsden's** is in a new building by the river, so you can watch the colourful little boats sailing past as you have a meal. It's perfect for a peaceful break during a busy day. Marsden's always serves traditional meat and fish dishes, and fantastic cakes and ice creams. People travel for miles to try them!

C **Violet's** is in an 18th-century house with a garden that's even large enough for a game of badminton! It's always lively and busy. Regular customers love it because they know they'll always find the same wonderful dishes there, and great desserts – such as cakes and ice creams, all at low prices!

D **Impey's** has large tables perfect for big groups of customers, both inside and in its garden. And even if you come here frequently, you'll still find new dishes on offer each week! Impey's is always busy, and has a great atmosphere – as well as fantastic artworks on its walls!

E As **Butterfly** is by the main cricket ground, it attracts local players who eat there in big groups after matches – it has lots of space inside. The unusual bright colours and huge art posters give it a cheerful atmosphere – great for meeting friends. The food's good, too, although it can be a bit expensive.

F The modern **Royale** café serves a range of tasty meals, including meat-free dishes. Surprisingly few people know about it, so you can stay in the peace of the little café and garden as long as you wish. Sunny yellow walls and fantastic art posters make it the happiest place in town!

G **Sands Café** usually attracts lots of people calling in after watching a game at the stadium nearby, because of its convenient location and lively atmosphere – and its delicious dishes, none of which cost a lot. You may even see famous players trying the fantastic hot meals!

H **Jerry's** is in one of the oldest streets in town, in what was once the town hall. Inside, you'll find lovely cream-coloured walls, comfortable sofas – and a great selection of books to entertain you as you eat their tasty sandwiches! The café also displays work by local painters and photographers.

Part 3

Questions 11–15

For each question, choose the correct answer.

Young birdwatcher

Fifteen-year-old Jana Green writes about her hobby of birdwatching.

I live in a house surrounded by beautiful countryside in Scotland. I've always loved nature and wild animals, and six years ago, I started a new hobby – birdwatching! I went to some mountains in northern Scotland with my family, where we saw lots of birds in their natural environment. I spent hours watching them with my parents, who showed me how to tell the difference between species and how to find the best places to see them. It was amazing, and after returning home, I joined a local young birdwatchers' club.

My goal is to see 200 different bird species, and I've almost achieved that because on family holidays abroad I've had the opportunity to see birds from other countries, too. We always look for places where there are group birdwatching activities, so I can add new birds to my list! I've been to Egypt, and last summer we went to South America, where I thought I'd have a good chance to see my 200th species. I wasn't too disappointed when it didn't happen, though, as I've learned that you have to be patient with this hobby.

I posted a video online about this challenge, and many teenagers enjoyed it and commented that it looked like a fascinating hobby. When my teachers saw it, they asked me to give a presentation about birdwatching to the school. I didn't feel nervous until just before they introduced me and I walked onto the stage. I knew I'd remember what to say and had some notes to help me, but the whole school and all my friends were watching me! I only relaxed when it was over and the teachers said I'd prepared well and they'd really enjoyed it. I might even do another one next year!

I'm lucky to live in the countryside. I understand why many teenagers in cities might not think of becoming birdwatchers, but there are actually plenty of birds to see, especially in places which have lots of green areas. I also think that birdwatching clubs should try to get more young people interested in this hobby. Everyone needs to connect with nature, whatever their age, and it doesn't have to cost much money.

11 How did Jana first become interested in birdwatching?

A She found that she was good at recognising different bird species.

B She was taught some birdwatching skills by her parents.

C She met some young people with a similar interest in birds.

D She moved to Scotland and discovered that she loved nature.

12 What does Jana say about her aim to see 200 bird species?

A She accepts that it might take longer than she had hoped.

B She is annoyed because she has not yet achieved this goal.

C She is certain she will soon see even more birds.

D She regrets that she has missed opportunities to see new birds.

13 How did Jana feel about giving her presentation?

A proud that the teachers had asked her to do it

B worried that she might forget the information

C anxious because the audience was so large

D confident that nothing could go wrong

14 What does Jana say about birdwatching in cities?

A Some cities plan to open birdwatching clubs for young people.

B There are more opportunities for birdwatching than people realise.

C Cities should have more parks in order to attract birds.

D It is hard to see a variety of bird species around cities.

15 What would Jana's parents say about Jana's hobby?

A Jana really enjoyed her birdwatching hobby when she was at her club, so it's a pity that she has given it up.

B Jana usually prefers us to go birdwatching on our own while we're on holiday.

C Jana gave a good presentation on birdwatching at her school, and has already given a second one.

D Jana's experience and love of birdwatching is encouraging other young people to become interested in this hobby.

Part 4

Questions 16–20

Five sentences have been removed from the text below.
For each question, choose the correct answer.
There are three extra sentences which you do not need to use.

Lost Irish beach returns after 33 years

Achill Island, off the coast of Ireland, is a popular tourist destination. It has beautiful mountains and clean beaches. The island was suddenly in the news in 1984 because of something that happened near the village of Dooagh. **16** _____ They discovered that their beach had disappeared during the night, leaving behind just rocks. For years after that, only small amounts of sand returned to the once-beautiful shore, and fewer and fewer tourists went there. **17** _____ The effect of this was felt by everyone in the small community.

Then, in 2017, something incredible happened. People couldn't believe their eyes when, one morning, they found that their beach had returned, and the rocks were once again covered in soft golden sand! **18** _____ They said that the amount of sand under the sea near the coast had slowly increased. Then, during a period of strong winds and powerful waves, most of it was carried to the shore.

The people of the island were of course delighted to have their beach back, and for some time, it attracted hundreds of visitors. **19** _____ Business owners in the area were also hopeful that the beach would encourage surfers to return to the region, making it a popular holiday destination again. **20** _____ No one was sure whether it was absolutely safe.

Later, a special type of seaweed – a plant that grows in the sea – appeared on the beach. It is traditionally used to help crops grow, so its return was particularly good news. The local people are hopeful that now the sand is finally here to stay.

A	They were able to experience these amazing events.
B	At first, however, people were advised to avoid going into the sea.
C	Losing so many visitors meant that many hotels and restaurants had to close.
D	But a most surprising thing happened that night.
E	Scientists from an Irish university provided a possible explanation.
F	Despite these benefits to plants and animals, a few people were disappointed.
G	One morning, the people living there had a nasty shock.
H	Tourists wanted to see the power of nature for themselves.

Part 5

Questions 21–26

For each question, choose the correct answer.

A popular song

Yesterday, a song by the British group The Beatles, is one of the world's most popular English-language songs. Originally **(21)** .... by The Beatles in 1965, a huge range of artists have created over 2,000 other **(22)** .... of the song since it was written. In 2000, customers of an international music video channel **(23)** .... to choose the best pop song of all time, and *Yesterday* won.

According to the writer of the song, Paul McCartney, the tune for the whole song came to him in a dream. When he woke up, he immediately played it on a piano to **(24)** .... forgetting it.

McCartney found writing words for the song more challenging than writing the music. When he first played it to the other **(25)** .... of the band, he still hadn't written any words. So he sang 'Scrambled eggs' instead of 'Yesterday'. Over 50 years later, *Yesterday* has **(26)** .... up being one of the world's most popular songs!

21	**A** designed	**B** invented	**C** recorded	**D** copied
22	**A** varieties	**B** forms	**C** types	**D** versions
23	**A** voted	**B** picked	**C** supported	**D** approved
24	**A** fail	**B** prevent	**C** miss	**D** avoid
25	**A** assistants	**B** partners	**C** members	**D** colleagues
26	**A** come	**B** ended	**C** set	**D** turned

Part 6

Questions 27–32

For each question, write the correct answer.
Write **one** word for each gap.

Match report: National Schools Tournament

by William Jacobs, football captain

Last Saturday, our school football team took part in the National Schools Tournament. It was a long day – we got to school very early as the bus **(27)** .... would take us to the tournament had to leave by 7 a.m. **(28)** .... an hour's drive we arrived at the City Stadium, where the competition was taking **(29)** .... Playing in such **(30)** .... famous stadium was an experience we will never forget.

We played against some of the top teams from around the country, and we came first! This was amazing because the other teams were much stronger this year **(31)** .... they were last year.

We were given our prize, a beautiful silver cup, and then we went on a tour around the stadium. We all agreed that it **(32)** .... been an incredible day, and we hope to be able to return next year!

WRITING (45 minutes)

Part 1

You **must** answer this question.
Write your answer in about **100 words** on the answer sheet.

Question 1

Read this email from your English-speaking friend Lennie and the notes you have made.

EMAIL

From: Lennie

Subject: Water sports centre

Thanks for inviting me to the water sports centre at the lake with you and your family tomorrow. I'm so excited about it – are you? — *Yes!*

I'm really looking forward to going sailing in the morning, and I know there's time to do something else in the afternoon. Would you like to try water skiing? — *No, because …*

You said we're going to a restaurant for a meal with your parents afterwards. What clothes should I bring to change into? — *Suggest …*

What time are we getting back in the evening? I need to tell my mum. — *Tell Lennie*

Let me know.

Lennie

Write your **email** to Lennie using **all the notes**.

Part 2

Choose **one** of these questions.
Write your answer in about **100 words** on the answer sheet.

Question 2

You see this announcement on an English-language website for young people.

Articles wanted!

Photos

Why do you think people take so many photos?

What do you like taking photos of?

Do you have a favourite photo that you look at often?

The best articles answering these questions will be published next month.

Write your **article**.

Question 3

Your English teacher has asked you to write a story.
Your story must begin with this sentence.

Chris and Jo were walking through the park when they saw a beautiful little box under a tree.

Write your **story**.

LISTENING (approximately 30 minutes)

Part 1

Questions 1–7

For each question, choose the correct answer.

---

1 How did they reach the top of the mountain?

A

B

C

2 What does the girl decide to do her project about?

A

B

C

3 What did the girl do last night?

A

B

C

4 Which food does the boy want to order?

A

B

C

5 What must students take to school tomorrow?

A

B

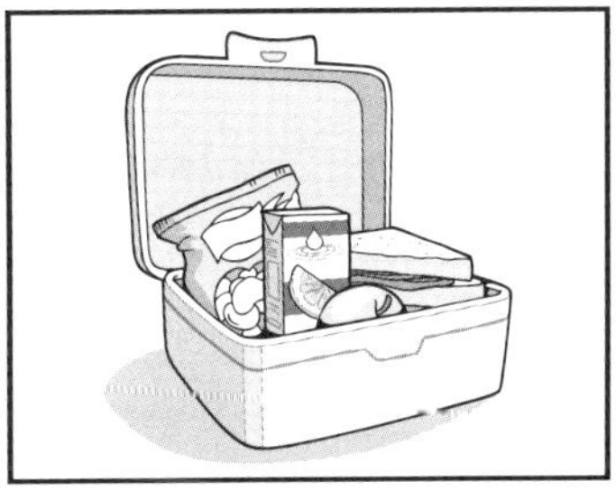

C

6 Which book does the boy decide to buy?

A

B

C

7 How will the friends get to the skateboard park?

A

B

C

Part 2

Questions 8–13

For each question, choose the correct answer.

---

8 You will hear two friends talking about a basketball match.
The boy says that his team

A played better than expected.

B nearly won the match.

C had the best players.

9 You will hear two friends talking about a new cinema.
They would both like the cinema to

A show more good films.

B have a bigger screen.

C open earlier in the day.

10 You will hear two friends talking about a sailing lesson.
How did the girl feel about it?

A pleased that the weather conditions were so good

B surprised by the progress she made

C happy that the instructor helped her

11 You will hear two friends talking about a TV talent competition.
The girl is going to enter it because she wants

A people to see her talent.

B to become famous.

C to win the prize.

12 You will hear a boy talking to a girl about books.
What is the boy doing?

A encouraging her to read a wider variety of books

B recommending a particular book to her

C offering to lend her a book

13 You will hear two friends talking about a video game.
The boy thinks that it

A is enjoyable to play in a group

B is easy after lots of practice.

C is suitable for young children.

Part 3

Questions 14–19

For each question, write the correct answer in the gap.
Write **one** or **two words** or a **number** or a **date** or a **time**.

You will hear a teacher telling students about a class camping trip.

Class camping trip

Time the coach leaves on Saturday: at **(14)** .... a.m.

Students must bring: a **(15)** ....

Place for students' meals at the campsite: a **(16)** ....

Students will visit: a **(17)** ....

Entertainment on the last day: a **(18)** ....

Address for the trip website: www. **(19)** .... .trip.org

Part 4

Questions 20–25

For each question, choose the correct answer.

You will hear an interview with a girl called Karina Wells, who is a member of a gymnastics club.

20 At her first gymnastics lesson, Karina felt

A pleased with the progress she made.

B surprised at how many people there were.

C worried that everyone else was better than her.

21 Karina says that her school friends often

A tell her to stop talking about gymnastics.

B try to copy the things she can do.

C ask her for advice about exercise.

22 At competitions, Karina is surprised that competitors

A are friendly with each other.

B make very few mistakes.

C feel so nervous.

23 Karina usually does her homework

A just before she goes to bed.

B on the way to the gym.

C straight after school.

24 Karina says she'd like to be able to eat

A the same as the rest of her family.

B a wider variety of dishes.

C more sweet food.

25 Karina thinks that doing gymnastics has taught her to

A help people more.

B make good use of her time.

C work well in a team.

56100

OFFICE USE ONLY - DO NOT WRITE OR MAKE ANY MARK ABOVE THIS LINE

Cambridge Assessment English

Candidate Name		Candidate Number	
Centre Name		Centre Number	
Examination Title		Examination Details	
Candidate Signature		Assessment Date	

Supervisor: If the candidate is ABSENT or has WITHDRAWN shade here ○

Preliminary for Schools Reading Candidate Answer Sheet

Instructions

Use a PENCIL (B or HB)

Rub out any answer you want to change with an eraser.

For Parts 1, 2, 3, 4 and 5:

Mark ONE letter for each answer.

For example: If you think A is the right answer to the question, mark your answer sheet like this:

0	A ●	B ○	C ○

Part 1			
1	A ○	B ○	C ○
2	A ○	B ○	C ○
3	A ○	B ○	C ○
4	A ○	B ○	C ○
5	A ○	B ○	C ○

Part 2								
6	A ○	B ○	C ○	D ○	E ○	F ○	G ○	H ○
7	A ○	B ○	C ○	D ○	E ○	F ○	G ○	H ○
8	A ○	B ○	C ○	D ○	E ○	F ○	G ○	H ○
9	A ○	B ○	C ○	D ○	E ○	F ○	G ○	H ○
10	A ○	B ○	C ○	D ○	E ○	F ○	G ○	H ○

Part 3				
11	A ○	B ○	C ○	D ○
12	A ○	B ○	C ○	D ○
13	A ○	B ○	C ○	D ○
14	A ○	B ○	C ○	D ○
15	A ○	B ○	C ○	D ○

Part 4								
16	A ○	B ○	C ○	D ○	E ○	F ○	G ○	H ○
17	A ○	B ○	C ○	D ○	E ○	F ○	G ○	H ○
18	A ○	B ○	C ○	D ○	E ○	F ○	G ○	H ○
19	A ○	B ○	C ○	D ○	E ○	F ○	G ○	H ○
20	A ○	B ○	C ○	D ○	E ○	F ○	G ○	H ○

Part 5				
21	A ○	B ○	C ○	D ○
22	A ○	B ○	C ○	D ○
23	A ○	B ○	C ○	D ○
24	A ○	B ○	C ○	D ○
25	A ○	B ○	C ○	D ○
26	A ○	B ○	C ○	D ○

Continues over →

OFFICE USE ONLY - DO NOT WRITE OR MAKE ANY MARK BELOW THIS LINE

56100

56100

OFFICE USE ONLY - DO NOT WRITE OR MAKE ANY MARK ABOVE THIS LINE

For Part 6:
Write your answers clearly in the spaces next to the numbers (27 to 32) like this:

0 ENGLISH

Write your answers in CAPITAL LETTERS.

Part 6		Do not write below here
27		27 1 0 ○ ○
28		28 1 0 ○ ○
29		29 1 0 ○ ○
30		30 1 0 ○ ○
31		31 1 0 ○ ○
32		32 1 0 ○ ○

OFFICE USE ONLY - DO NOT WRITE OR MAKE ANY MARK BELOW THIS LINE

56100

You must write within the grey lines.

Write your answer for Part 1 below. Do not write on the barcodes.

Question 1

This section for use by Examiner only:

C	CA	O	L

* 0010446611102 *

You must write within the grey lines.

Answer only one of the two questions for Part 2.
Tick the box to show which question you have answered.
Write your answer below. Do not write on the barcodes.

Part 2	**Question 2** ☐	**Question 3** ☐

This section for use by Examiner only:

C	CA	O	L

* 0010446611103 *

40787

OFFICE USE ONLY - DO NOT WRITE OR MAKE ANY MARK ABOVE THIS LINE

Page 1 of 1

Cambridge Assessment English

Candidate Name		Candidate Number	
Centre Name		Centre Number	
Examination Title		Examination Details	
Candidate Signature		Assessment Date	

Supervisor: If the candidate is ABSENT or has WITHDRAWN shade here O

Preliminary for Schools Listening Candidate Answer Sheet

Instructions

Use a PENCIL (B or HB). Rub out any answer you want to change with an eraser.

For Parts 1, 2 and 4:
Mark one letter for each answer. For example: If you think **A** is the right answer to the question, mark your answer sheet like this:

0	A ●	B O	C O

For Part 3:
Write your answers clearly in the spaces next to the numbers (14 to 19) like this:

0	ENGLISH

Write your answers in CAPITAL LETTERS.

Part 1	A	B	C
1	O	O	O
2	O	O	O
3	O	O	O
4	O	O	O
5	O	O	O
6	O	O	O
7	O	O	O

Part 2	A	B	C
8	O	O	O
9	O	O	O
10	O	O	O
11	O	O	O
12	O	O	O
13	O	O	O

Part 3		Do not write below here
14		14 1 O 0 O
15		15 1 O 0 O
16		16 1 O 0 O
17		17 1 O 0 O
18		18 1 O 0 O
19		19 1 O 0 O

Part 4	A	B	C
20	O	O	O
21	O	O	O
22	O	O	O
23	O	O	O
24	O	O	O
25	O	O	O

OFFICE USE ONLY - DO NOT WRITE OR MAKE ANY MARK BELOW THIS LINE

Page 1 of 1

40787

Acknowledgements

The authors and publishers acknowledge the following sources of copyright material and are grateful for the permissions granted. While every effort has been made, it has not always been possible to identify the sources of all the material used, or to trace all copyright holders. If any omissions are brought to our notice, we will be happy to include the appropriate acknowledgements on reprinting and in the next update to the digital edition, as applicable.

Key: RT = Reading Test, ST = Speaking Test

Photography

The following photographs have been sourced from Getty Images.

RT1: Jasmin Merdan/Moment; Rajesh Mhatre/EyeEm; nuiiko/iStock/Getty Images Plus; Juanmonino/iStock/Getty Images Plus; kate_sept2004/E+; **RT2:** Compassionate Eye Foundation/Martin Barraud/Stone; SDI Productions/E+; Juanmonino/E+; Kentaroo Tryman/Maskot; Compassionate Eye Foundation/Jetta Productions/Photodisc; **RT3:** Jasmin Merdan/Moment; Yasser Chalid/Moment; brusinski/iStock/Getty Images Plus; Maskot/DigitalVision; HRAUN/E+; **RT4:** JGI/Jamie Grill; Jose Luis Pelaez Inc/DigitalVision/Getty Images Plus; ER Productions Limited/DigitalVision; Robert Daly/OJO Images; shapecharge/E+; **ST1:** fstop123/E+; Westend61; **ST2:** Â© Hello Lovely/Corbis; mixetto/E+; **ST3:** Anchiy/E+; PamelaJoeMcFarlane/E+; **ST4:** monkeybusinessimages/iStock/Getty Images Plus; Carlo A/The Image Bank.

Illustrations

Cambridge University Press & Assessment.

Audio

Audio production by dsound recording studios.

Typesetting

Typeset by QBS Learning.

Visual materials for the Speaking test

Test 1

Part 2

Task 1A

Task 1B

Test 1

Part 3

Task 1C

Different ways to improve English skills

Test 2

Part 2

Task 2A

Task 2B

Test 2

Part 3

Task 2C

Things the library could have

Test 3

Part 2

Task 3A

Task 3B

Test 3

Part 3

Task 3C

Places to celebrate a birthday

Test 4

Part 2

Task 4A

Task 4B

Test 4

Part 3

Task 4C

Prizes for a volleyball competition

Calaimage/Sam Edwards/Getty In